BOYS GUIDE TO PUBERTY & BODY CARE

NEW Edition

GROWING UP BOOK FOR AGES 8-12

Natalia Spark

TABLE OF CONTENTS

1

You are Growing Up

Growing up happens when your body undergoes various changes as you move from a child to a teenager and, eventually, an adult.

Hormones produced in the brain are responsible for the body changes during this growth spurt

These Hormones travel through your body to your testicles, stimulating your body to start producing sperm.

Body changes will happen gradually over a long period:

Growing up Could Also Be a Fun Time Too

You could play the guitar, sing a song, go out playing football, or dream of becoming a doctor.

These might seem like a lot. it's perfectly normal because all boys go through this stage too.

You will become taller, gain lots of muscle mass, along side a broad shoulder. During this time, boys grow nearly an inch (9.5 cm) per year on average. Boys have a later growth spurt in late stages than girls.

Puberty involves **hairs** growing on your chest, arms, legs, armpits, and face as well.

- Due to the positive association between vitamin D and testosterone levels, more sunlight exposure for a guy is likely to increase testosterone levels.

- Cuddling and other acts of love have been shown to speed up the healing of physical wounds by releasing Oxytocin, which has been shown to minimize swelling.

Vitamin D is the only vitamin that also functions as a hormone. Its shortage can lead to a variety of mental diseases, including depression and schizophrenia.

Our bodies are special and it has many parts.

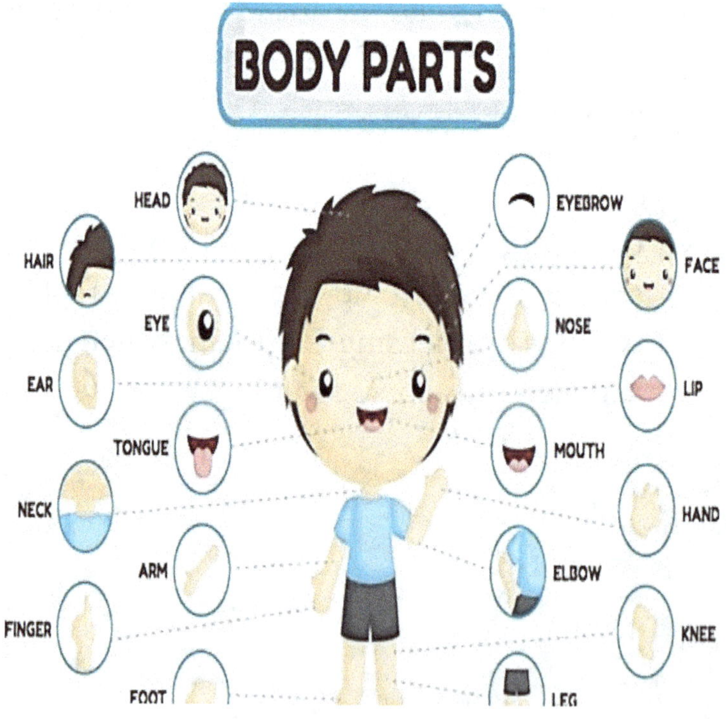

Several changes occur and your growth slows down as you reach the end of puberty. Your height and genital organs will develop more body hair and become more muscular.

Changes to look out For:

More sweating. Since sweat can cause body odour, taking a bath or shower every day is beneficial.

Acne (pimples). Always wash your face in the morning and at night with fragrance-free soap and water.

Voice changes : the voice cracks occasionally. This is because your larynx (voice box) is expanding. Almost every part, including the larynx, participates in the growing action.

The larynx is also known as the voice box, and it is located in the throat. The larynx is responsible for giving you a voice, whether you're talking, laughing, whispering, singing, or shouting. Humming and touching

The larynx is seen at the front of the throat. It grows in size during puberty; it protrudes from the front of the throat. This is the Adam's apple. This explains why boys have Adam's apples. Most Girls do not have Adam's apples, but some do. In any case, it's not a big deal.

But why is it called Adam's apple? *was it named after the Garden of Eden story in which Adam ate a piece of the forbidden fruit that became lodged in his throat? Adam's apple can appear as a small, rounded apple just under the skin in front of the throat.*

Boys have deeper voices becomes deeper due to their larger larynx. As girls' larynxes grow larger, their voices become a little deeper.

Attraction. Young boys develop a growing attraction towards the opposite sex.

Growth Spurts

For girls, the average age to begin puberty is around 8 years old for girls and 10 years old for boys. However, it are earlier or later — between the ages of 7 and 13 for girls and 9 and 15 for boys.

Around a year or so after your body shows the first

signs of puberty as the penis and testicles starts growing bigger.

Hormones are responsible for most of these body changes. The process of growing up continues all through the teenage years.

now you will start to look less like a kid and more like a grown-up.

Do you have more questions ? We are here to give some answers to commonly asked questions

Young boys grow tall during puberty. Your genetic makeup will largely determine your overall height.

Growth spurts mean big, quick increases in height. During a growth spurt, you will grow several inches in a very short time. This is quite normal.

Don't worry if you notice that you are not growing as tall as some of your friends or that you are growing taller than some of your friends since your genes determine how tall you will become.

It's OK that some girls your age might grow quite taller than you since they experience puberty earlier than boys. Overall, any changes in height that you experience are mostly normal, and there is little to nothing you can do about it. So, do not stress over it.

You may notice that some of your friends are already developing muscles in the chest area and even developing broad shoulders, but not you yet.

Do not worry, it will happen soon.

Get some rest!

After working, you get some rest. This rejuvenates and re-energizes the body.

To Do List

2

Hormones and Growing Up

What are hormones?

Hormones are chemical substances, which interact with the organs, skin, muscles, and other tissues to coordinate various tasks in the body. They send signals telling the body on what to do and when to do it.

Hormones regulate a wide range of body functions, including:

✓ **Development and growth.**

✓ **Sexual activity.**

✓ **Reproduction.**

✓ **The sleep-wake cycle**

 **Mood.**

Hormones work on a specific part of the body — this happens when the cells in the target tissue have receptors that receive the hormone's message. hormone act as keys, and the cells of its target tissue, to be specially formed locks.

- The pituitary gland is the most important gland during puberty. It's a tiny gland (located at the base of the brain) instructs other glands on how to function.
- The pituitary gland is also responsible for the human brain's development.
- Growth hormone makes bones and muscles grow bigger and stronger.
- Hormones are also responsible for sexual reproduction.

Some of the changes occur only in boys, while others occur in both boys and girls.

HORMONES

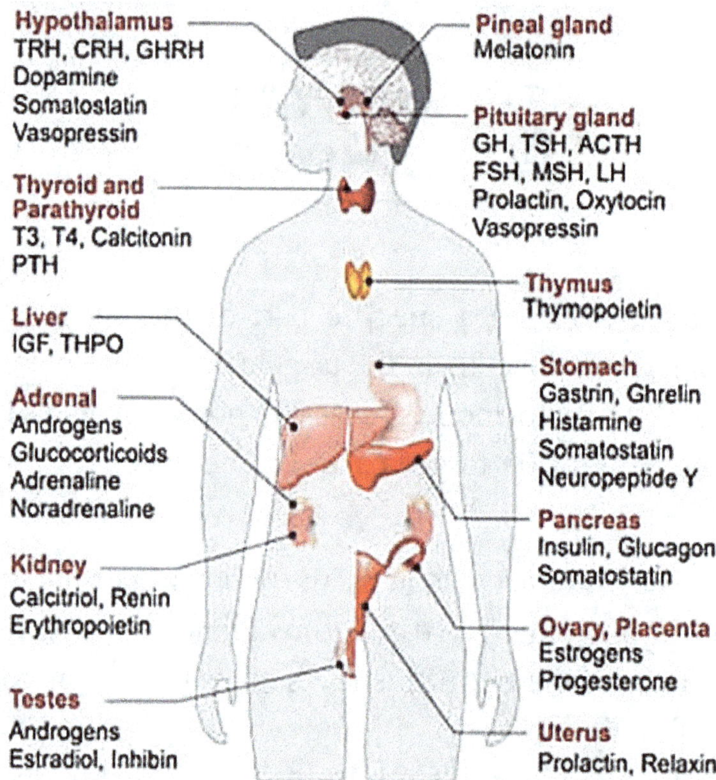

You'll need to start paying attention to yourself once you hit puberty.

These changes are a natural aspect of maturing into an adult. Continue reading to learn more about growing up.

3

Personal Hygiene and Body Care

Good hygiene is essential for staying healthy. Poor hygiene spreads bacteria to other parts of your body, causing illness. Fortunately, maintaining good

hygiene is easier when you keep yourself clean and develop good habits.

Germs can remain on your hands for up to three hours.

Your fingertips and elbows contain between 2 and 10 million germs.

Without washing your hands, you transfer germs to the food and beverages you consume.

When your hands are damp, they distribute 1,000 times more germs than when they are dry.

A germ is a microscopic creature that is capable of causing disease and illness. Germs get on to your hands after using the restroom, changing a diaper, handling raw meats, or touching any germ-infested object. When your hands germy, Wash them with soap to get rid of bacteria.

nobody enjoys being ill, and some of these illnesses are pretty serious. Second, those who become ill may suffer financial consequences.

The sweat glands produce sweat. Sweat is one of the means through which your body passes metabolic wastes in the form of water through your skin.

The bacteria on your skin act upon the water molecules and salt. This is what causes the smell and body odour of boys.

To keep yourself from being smelly, after sweating, do the following:

Have a Good Bath

1. A good soap and hot water will be sufficient. Focus on the face, hands, feet, underarms, groin, and bottom.

Wash your hair

Wash your hair daily, especially when it's coarse and dry. If you have extremely greasy, oily, or fine hair, however, do it every day to avoid oil build-up.

Trim your nails.

Trim your nails when they get too long. Also, wash them when you wash your hands to keep them clean. Keeping good nail hygiene is easier with shorter nails.

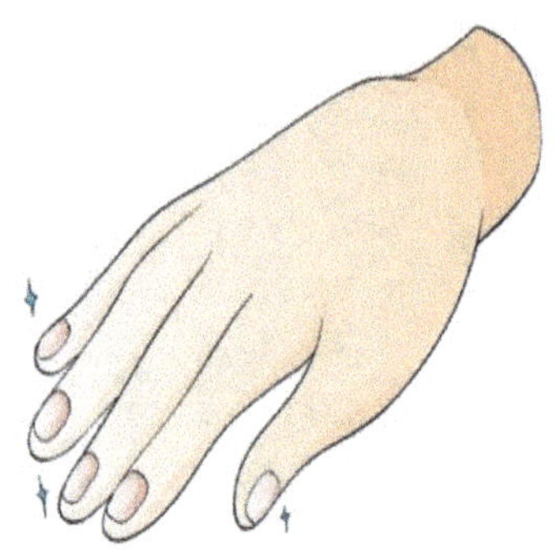

Wear clean clothes.

Dirty clothes can make bacteria can accumulate in the body. It's good to change your underwear or undershirts, which you wear always.

Your parents, go to the store and buy some deodorant for you. Apply deodorant to your underarms every day when you wake up to keep them smelling fresh throughout the day.

Your feet might smell if you wear dirty socks or no socks at all. When this happens, try cleaning your feet when you shower or bathe, and rotate which shoes you

wear during the week.

Dry them before wearing socks and shoes. You might apply talcum powder to your feet so they smell good.

Daily Hygiene Routine

Getting up at 7 a.m. to brush your teeth, wash your face, and apply deodorant before going to school is a simple morning routine. You could shower at 6 p.m. and brush and floss your teeth right before bed when you get home.

If your face appears to be oily, wash it with a facial soap designed for oily skin.

Always wash your hands after using the restroom, playing outside, or handling anything that may contain bacteria. To avoid getting sick or spreading germs to the food you're eating, wash your hands before and after eating.

Body Hair

body hair appears in areas like your face, your armpit, your pubic region, and sometimes your chest and legs. These are signs of puberty, and they are perfectly normal.

The hair under your arms (armpits) and on your face may grow at the same time during puberty.

The last hairs to grow will be on your chin. If you let your chin hair grow fully, you will have a beard.

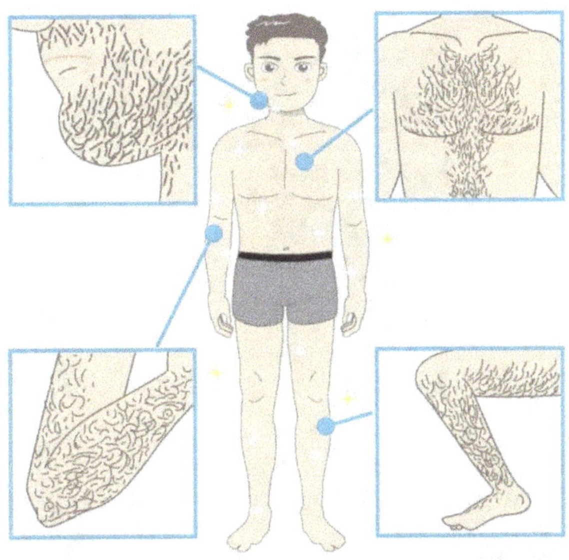

Apply shaving gel or foam before you shave.

This is especially important if you have sensitive skin or if you get a lot of spots when you shave. If you haven't had to deal with this yourself, check out our advice on shaving with acne, because we know how to do it.

Practice Shaving Weekly

There are a few things to do before your first shave.

☞ Always shave in the direction of hair growth to avoid shaving bumps.

☞ Remember to always change the blade frequently. If you do not, the blade will become dull and blunt, and it's likely to cause shaving bumps that way.

☞ While shaving, bumps, and cuts sometimes occur.

☞ When the skin becomes irritated with red bumps or an itchy rash, you have a skin condition called folliculitis from shaving.

4

Taking Good Care of Your Teeth

Bacteria and germs grow on your teeth when there are food particles in our mouth . These germs cause bleeding and bad breath.

Always brush your teeth every morning and more often (for example, if you have braces). Daily cleaning makes your teeth and gums healthy.

Brush your teeth at least twice per day, and floss at least once per day. Toothpaste contains chemicals, such as fluorides, which help prevent cavities in the teeth.

Interesting facts about teeth

- ✓ There are 20 teeth in the initial set of teeth (baby teeth).
- ✓ There are 32 teeth in the second set of teeth (adult teeth).The teeth is the only portion of the human body that cannot repair itself . They're covered in enamel, which isn't alive.
- ✓ The Tooth enamel is the toughest part in the human body, its harder than the bone.
- ✓ The average person spends 38 days brushing their teeth in their lifetime.
- ✓ Under your gums, one-third of your teeth are located.
- ✓ Humans only acquire two sets of teeth in their lifetime, but dolphins get one (monophyodont) and some have many sets (polyphyodont); sharks get over 40.

Toothpaste contains abrasives, detergents, and foaming agents, which ensures a healthy tooth.

Brushing gets rid of bacteria that causes bad breath.

If your teeth are sensitive to heat, cold, and pressure, you may want to carefully select your toothpaste designed for sensitive heat.

2. Your toothbrush should be held at an angle of 45 degrees against your gums. Then, gently brush from the junction between your teeth and your gums to the surfaces of your teeth.

3. Use the same angle of 45 degrees from the teeth-gum junction to the surface method to brush all the outside and inside surfaces of your teeth.

3. Hold the toothbrush vertically and, with gentle strokes, brush the inside surfaces of your top and bottom front teeth and gums.

4. For the tongue, use a forward-rapid motion but with some gentleness to brush the surface. This will effectively get rid of the metabolizing bacteria on it.

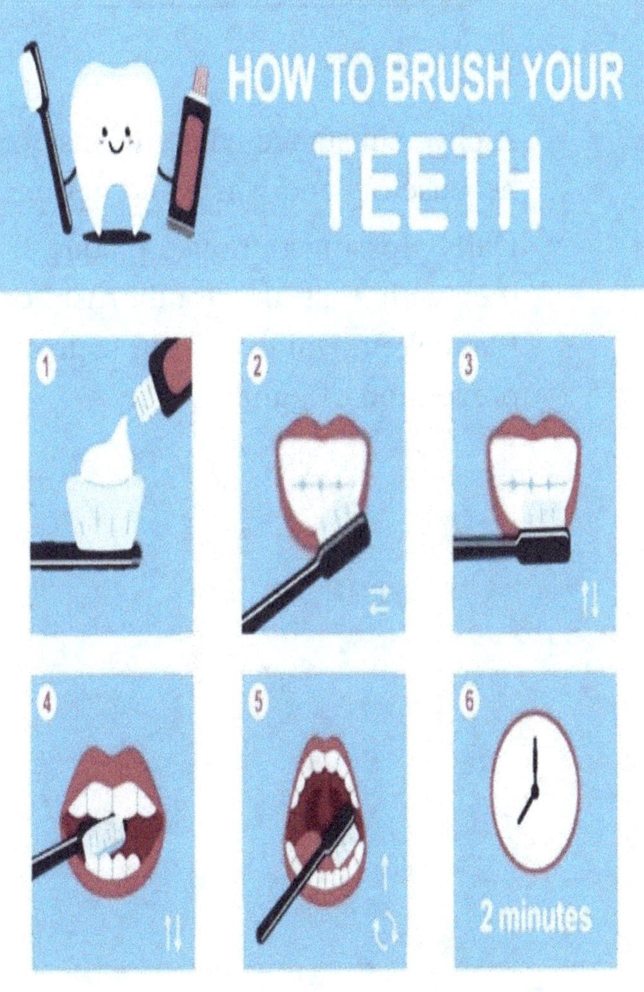

✓ Brushing your teeth twice a day, removes the plaque that causes cavities. Plaque is a soft,

sticky substance that forms on the teeth because of food waste and germs.

✓ Daily flossing removes plaque from between the teeth that the toothbrush cannot reach. Plaque removal from your teeth also aids in the prevention of gum disease.

5

What's happening down there?

As a young boy, your penis and scrotum are sensitive

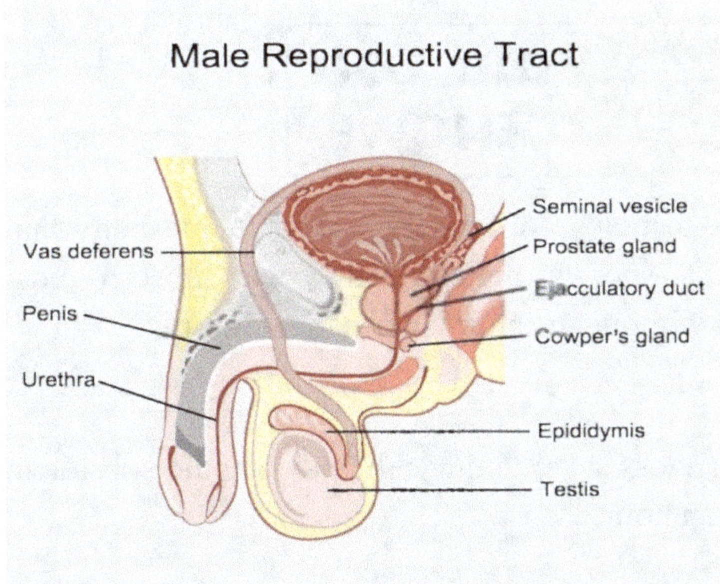

parts of your body. So what's happening "down there"?

The scrotum is a bag that contains two tiny organs known as testicles.

This area also has many nerve endings, making it especially sensitive, so if a soccer ball whams into a boy in that spot, it hurts a lot.

Unfortunately, you can injure the penis when playing with your friends, riding a bike or engaging in sports. It is also possible when someone bumps or kicks you down there.

The good news is that these injuries are usually not serious, but they may cause pain in a short period.

Since the testicles are closely linked to the body and made of a spongy material, they can absorb most accidents without sustaining permanent injury.

If there is a less severe injury, the pain should subside in less than an hour.

What If I Am Ashamed?

Young boys are sometimes ashamed of telling anyone about their penis, testicles, or scrotum. You do not have to — if you feel strange down there, you might open to your dad. When that's not possible, let your mom know.

Sperm cells are quite tiny....

Have you ever wondered what the size of these hidden swimmers is? Sperm cells, on the other hand, are extremely small. They are, in fact, some of the smallest cells in the human body, measuring only 0.005cm. To put things into perspective, scientists require a 400x magnification microscope to see a sperm cell. This is a stark contrast to the female egg cell, which, ironically, is one of the largest cells in the human body and are seen with the naked eye... They claim that opposites attract!

2. They may be little, but they are numerous!

What sperm cells lack in size, they make up for in quantity. If the sperm count is normal, each male ejaculation comprises tens of millions of sperm, with up to 100 million new cells being created every day. That's a lot of sperm.

The male reproductive system is comprised of the penis, scrotum, and testicles, as well as a variety of internal accessory organs such as the prostate gland and seminal vesicles, which produce all fluids.

Reproductive cells of various sizes is found in the reproductive system.

They come in many shapes and sizes and perform a variety of functions.

The sperm measures only 5 micrometres by 3 micrometres when you include the sperm's "tail". By comparison, the diameter of a red blood cell is approximately 8 micrometres, or approximately a tenth of the diameter of a human hair.

When cleaning, use a gentle soap and warm water.

Lift the scrotum and pull back the foreskin to wash every portion.

Clean the base of the penis and the testicles as well, where sweat and hair congregate.

Clean the area between the base of the testicles and the anus when washing.

Do this once a day.

3. Thoroughly dry

After washing, be sure to dry well with a dry cloth.

4. Wear a clean underwear

Make sure to wash your underwear on a regular basis with a mild detergent.

Wearing unclean underwear causes bad odours and encourages bacteria growth around your penis.

At least twice a day, you should change your underwear.

6

Getting Help From School

Doing your homework is an opportunity to practice what you have learnt in school.

Asking your parents or elderly relatives, for help with your homework is perfectly normal.

You will find information on the internet that will supply you with more than you need.

Do not copy the information and answers you see on the internet. Try reading, and when you have understood, then answer your questions based on what you have read.

Homework helps young children develop fundamental skills that will serve them throughout their school and working lives. Grade improvement, discipline, time management, resource management, and communication improvement are all critical life skills that will open doors to unique opportunities and assist children in finding success in their careers. Regular homework completion should be viewed as a financial investment in your child's future.

1. Practice Discipline

While repetition of a task may seem tedious, it is necessary to help your child develop his or her skill and understanding of a subject. Regular homework will help students understand certain concepts and will put them in a better position to pursue a vocational career.

2. Manage Your Time

Beyond the task itself, homework teaches children to manage their workload and improves their time management skills. Homework is assigned with a deadline, and students who take ownership of this deadline develop their ability to think independently and solve problems. This is an excellent illustration of why homework is necessary, as time management is a critical life skill that will benefit children throughout their higher education and careers.

3. Effective Communication

Homework serves as a bridge, allowing teachers and parents to gain a better understanding of how students learn, resulting in a more nuanced understanding of how to approach their learning and development. Many parents also desire that their child receive homework in order for them to comprehend what they are learning in school.

4. Aids learning At home

While classrooms are designed to be warm and inviting, there is no place like home. Homework provides students with an opportunity to learn and retain information in an environment that is most comfortable for them, which can aid in their development.

6. Discipline

Regular homework teaches children a pattern that will aid them in studying for important tests and exams. Children who are accustomed to completing homework on a regular basis will find it relatively easy to adapt to a schedule of regular revision at home. Access to learning materials, time management, and discipline all contribute to children revising more effectively and ultimately improving their grades.

Some boys enjoy doing their homework with friends and classmates in the neighbourhood.

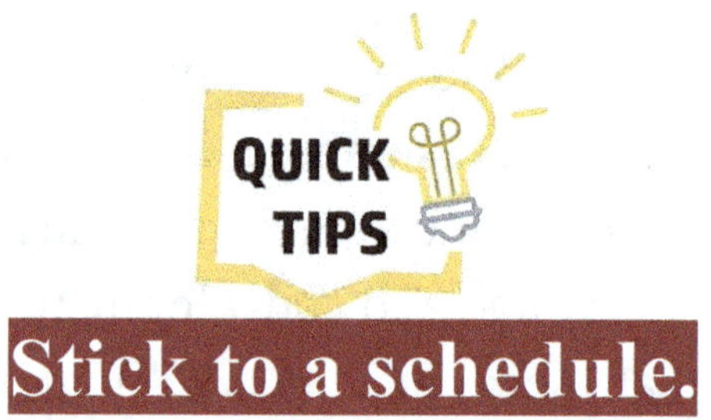

Stick to a schedule.

Some kids prefer to do their homework right after school, while others prefer to 'unwind' or eat first, then do their homework later. Make your decision, but make sure they stick to it.

3. Be Open to new ideas.

Do you love to study by yourself, or with your friends or family? You can work with music playing in the background to stay focused.

4. Go to the library

If you don't have enough space in the house to work, try a local library or a homework club at your child's school if one is available. Children can use computers at the library to access the internet if they don't have access at home.

5. Read aloud to one another

As a parent, you are your child's first teacher, and reading together is a great way to help your child learn, especially when they first start school. Even as they grow older, children enjoy being read to. Remember that both parents should share the storytelling duties, as fathers are powerful role models who have a significant impact on their sons' attitudes toward reading. Allow them to see you, as well as older children, reading.

6. Reward yourself

You can play with your friends whenever you have completed your homework.

7

Good Grades are Important

A good grade reflects both hard work and understanding of what you have learned. Working towards good grades gives you crucial skills in studying, preparation, discipline, and self-advocacy in the long run. These are life skills that will benefit you long after you stop taking math tests and writing book reports.

Students that get high marks are provided opportunities in secondary schools through organisations.

1. Plan Ahead

Stay on top of the material, write down and asked questions that arose from your reviews, and go over class and textbook notes to ensure you understand everything. Your last-minute review will be relatively leisurely and

organized, not feverish and harried. Therefore avoid "crash reading" at all costs.

2. Use the Alarm Clocks

If you have an upcoming exam early in the morning and you are afraid you won't be in shape for it, do a bit of subterfuge on your body and brain—get up early for several days before the exam, have a good breakfast, and do homework or review your notes. This will help jump-start your brain and get you used to the idea of solving equations or thinking seriously about Shakespeare at an earlier-than-usual hour.

Lastly, bring to the test whatever materials you need, from pens and pencils to calculators. I also recommend—taking notes as he's/she's reading a chapter. Learn to skim material, learn to study tables and charts.

- Summarize in the own words. Create your flashcards for a quick review of dates, formulas, and other information.

- Practise spelling words, etc.

Good grades boost your self-esteem.

Teenagers are sometimes hesitant to try hard because they are terrified of failing, so they give up and never attempt. What do you have to be terrified of?

Simply put in the best effort and you will see the benefits. In addition, it will make you perform better the next time. This will boost your confidence and allow you to take on additional academic challenges.

You can get a scholarship if you have good grades.

Isn't getting a scholarship worthwhile?

8

Making Friends That Care

Making friends is an important part of life. These are people you play games together. It's ok if you want to socialize more.

✓ Is someone you can count on.

✓ ... Is someone you can trust."

✓ Is considerate of your feelings.

✓ Listens when you need to talk.
Makes you feel good about yourself.

✓ Like some or many of the same things you do.

✓ May have some differences from you but it doesn't affect our relationship.

One way to make new friends is to find an activity you enjoy in which you might also meet new people. For example, if you enjoy music, try out for the school band. If you like sports, join a local team. If you are into art, find a local art center and join a group. Or just sit next to someone new at lunch or offer a bag of chips to someone to start a conversation.

To keep a good friend, you need to be a good friend yourself. Do you have these qualities? Look at the list of good friends we just had over. What do you expect from your friends? Are you as supportive of them as you'd like them to be of you?

Young boys are always searching for like-minded friends. If you ensure that you are there for your friends, chances are they will do the same for you.

Most disagreements between friends start over something small which builds into something bigger. For example, a fight might start when a friend teases you about getting a new haircut. At first, the teasing might seem only funny, but then you will start feeling annoyed and even embarrassed, especially if the teasing is happening in public. You may then start making fun of your friend in return. War of words may follow which may descend into real fights.

If you are not comfortable with some kind of teasing, politely tell your friends that you don't like being teased and that they should stop it. You can also just walk away or change the topic.

This happens as you get older and your interests change. It's hard to talk about growing apart, but it's better to talk it over than leave your old friend.

If this happens to you, concentrate on making some new friends or working on improving other friendships you have.

9

Learning About Consent and Boundaries

Boundaries are the personal boundaries we establish with others. They exemplify what we consider acceptable or unacceptable in other people's behaviour toward us. Establishing boundaries will keep you from getting hurt by others.

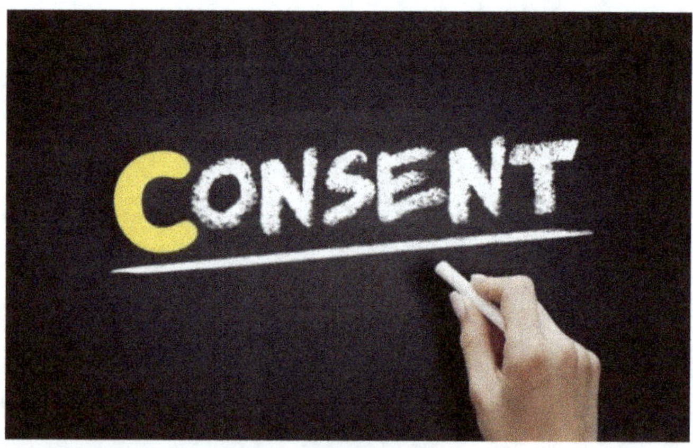

Consider boundaries as protective bubbles. This invisible bubble surrounds you and serves as both a physical and emotional "boundary."

This bubble can act as an impenetrable barrier to actions or words from others that we do not wish to receive. We

get to draw the line based on our values.

The concept of a bubble is important. The line we draw between others and ourselves is imaginary. However, most of us are aware of it when it is crossed.

The truth is that we teach others how to treat us. So, while it's easy to get irritated with people who repeatedly rub so hard against our bubble that it feels like it's about to burst, we're partly to blame for the situation if we remain silent.

We must establish healthy boundaries with ourselves before we can establish healthy boundaries with others.

Here are a few ways to protect your mental space that you can start doing right now!

- You are in charge of your body. You have control over how you interact with others and how others interact with you.
- You can do A high-five, blow a kiss, or simply say "Good Morning" if they do not want to hug during greetings and goodbyes.

- Always ask permission before touching others, and let them ask from you also.

☞ Report anyone who threatens you or tells you to keep secrets to these adults.

☞ Get permission before borrowing other people's items, posting photos online, making group plans, and, of course, touching others.

What is a crush?

Having romantic feelings toward another person. When you have a crush, you may find out that you are thinking about your crush all the time, or you may feel nervous as you are around them. These are all normal responses to having a crush and some people have it when they begin to experience puberty.

.

What not to do at this juncture is join bad gangs to get involved in immoral sexual activity.

Find out what your crush is interested in.

Find out what they are passionate about if you want to know someone. Find out what motivates them to work there, and see if you can volunteer together. This will keep them in good mood.

Nothing makes me more drawn to a crush than witnessing them smile over a cause or interest that they are truly passionate about. Inquiring about their priorities will not only get you closer to them, but will also help you comprehend the type of person they are.

Make direct eye contact.

If you like someone and are sitting across the table from them, make eye contact with them throughout your talk. You don't have to stare at them as they're shovelling food into their mouth, but you should avoid looking down when you're chatting, glancing about the room, or looking at your phone. If you glance away from them, you'll appear uninterested or indicate to your admirer that you'd rather be somewhere else. That is not what anyone wants! Furthermore, making eye contact will make you appear more confident, which will only make you appear more appealing to them.

It's a good idea to try to avoid regular contact with the person you've formed a crush on as part of the above procedure. Depending on who it is, this can be a easy process.

If it's someone we don't see very often, we can simply avoid them whenever feasible. However, if it's someone who is very much a part of our lives, try to stop meeting a certain group of friends as frequently.

10

Dealing With Peer Pressure.

What is peer pressure?

Your Peers are people your age who share certain things in common such as class, room, and so on. Your close friends (peers) do certain things together, like wearing similar types of clothing, visiting the same places, eating the same type of food, etc. When you influence each other to do something, this is referred to as "peer pressure. Peer pressure could be positive or negative.

Positive peers, includes the following ; Studying, being kind to older people, helping out at home, and avoiding alcohol and drugs. It is called Positive peer pressure.

Negative peer pressure

When someone tries to get you to do something that is bad. For example cheating, drinking alcohol, cutting class, lying to your parents, or shoplifting. This pressure may come or threats.

Do not be too quick to join a group or "fit in." bullies might make fun of you if you are not getting along.

The choices you make have a lasting impact (both positive and negative) on your future.

What if some of your friends have started behaving badly?

When you discover that some of your friends who you thought were well behaved have started engaging in illicit acts such as shoplifting, lying, or even using some illegal drugs. Deep down, you know that stealing is wrong and you don't want to get in trouble. Keep in mind that the consequences of shoplifting can have a lasting effect on you. Do not allow yourself to be pressured into doing something you know is wrong.

If your friends care about you, they will respect that you need to make your own decisions. Otherwise, they are not good for you anyway and cut you off from them. It's better to lose them as friends now and make new, better friends than to risk going to jail or earning a bad reputation for evil behaviour.

1) Did you know that 41% of all teenagers face peer pressure to be nasty to others? When did being mean become fashionable in school? The proverb "Do not do to others what you would not want done to you" dates all the way back thousands of years... If it has lasted this long, I suppose it is worth following.

2) If you're fortunate enough to obtain a car while still in your adolescence, it's a blast to show off your new automobile to your peers. However, conversing with and joking with friends while driving is risky. Did you know that 44% of kids drive better when they are alone in the car?

3) Peer pressure does not always have a bad connotation. Several are truly favourable. Although it occurs in fewer than half of the cases, positive peer pressure aids in the adoption of positive behaviours and the cessation of negative ones.

4) Sixty-seven percent of adolescent females are forced to dress a certain way. Allow no one to alter a style that suits you. However, it is always acceptable to seek the advice of close friends and family members regarding your attire.

What if some of my friends are trying to get me to try using drugs, alcohol, or cigarettes?

Just say no! in response to pressure to do something you know is wrong. You always have the choice to say, "No, I don't, do you want to do that "or" No, I don't feel like doing that, walk away from relationships, and harm your health.

let your friends know you are serious when you say "NO". it might also help them make better decisions and choices for themselves. Saying "NO" to peer pressure can also help you realize who your good friends are. Good friends will support your decisions and respect your feelings.

Again, avoid situations and events where teenagers might be drinking, using drugs, or doing other risky things.

In addition to saying "NO" to your friends who are trying to get you to do things, you know to do, Give your reasons for not doing them.

You can do many worthy things. Mention them

11

Dealing With Bullying

Bullying is the act of insulting, shaming other people, especially those of lesser privileges and power, using cruel words, gestures, or actions.

It involves comments or actions, which are physical

(in person) and online, bullying is a bad behaviour which must not be encouraged.

Bullies will be around you for a while, but they have no authority over you! You give them power over you if you fear them. Do not be afraid of the bully (do not refer to him as YOUR bully), you have many people on your side, and I'm pretty sure he has a lot more to fear if he tries to touch you. You are not on your own. Be strong!

What Should You Do If You're Being Bullied?

In a calm, clear voice, look at the kid who is bullying you and tell him or her to stop. Alternatively, you can try to laugh it off. If joking comes naturally to you, this will work best. It has the potential to catch the kid who is bullying you off guard.

If speaking up seems too difficult or dangerous, walk away and do not come back. Do not retaliate. Locate an adult who can intervene immediately to stop the bullying.

Keep your distance from places where bullying occurs.

Keep an eye out for adults and other children. When adults aren't present, the majority of bullying occurs.

Cyberbullying: How to Avoid It

Cyberbullying is a form of bullying that takes place online, via text messages, or email. There are steps you can take to safeguard yourself.

Being kind to people online will help you stay safe. Do not say anything that causes pain to others.

Be careful of what you post on the internet. Strangers, to be sure. Friends? What about friends of friends? You can control who sees what by using privacy settings.

Let your parents what you are up to on the internet and with whom you're doing it. Allow them to become your friend or follow you. Pay attention to what they have to say about what is and is not acceptable behaviour. They care about you and want you to be safe.

There are safe things you can do to stop bullying when you see it.

Get permission before posting anything about a friend, such as a photo or a video.

12

Social Media Tips

Social media is all about Sending messages via instant messaging over the Internet or between smartphones (e.g., Facebook Messenger, iMessage, WhatsApp, Hangouts).

Social media sites help us send messages in a variety of ways. Information sent to the Facebook wall may be visible to the public, or only to friends or followers, depending on your user privacy settings.

Photo and Video Sharing

Users can upload photos and videos, as well as share live videos, on many social networking sites and apps. Depending on the privacy settings, these are public or private.

Vlogs: Short for "video blogs," vlogs are video blogs that are posted regularly to a video sharing platform (such as YouTube)

Creating and Joining Groups: Many apps allow you to create and join groups. To access information and have conversations with other members, people "join," "like," or "follow" groups.

Children and teenagers go online to play games, either alone or with their friends. Free online gambling is available in some apps, and many others feature product promotion or advertising.

Online Dating: Numerous apps and websites assist strangers in making romantic or sexual connections over the internet.

- Understand the programs and apps.

- On the Internet, it is easy for someone to pretend to be someone they aren't.

- Meeting an online friend in person must take place in a public place and with a trusted adult.

- Do not post anything on social media that you would not want your parents or teachers to see or read. Because information and photos obtained from the internet are found years later,

While social media are exciting, it should be viewed as a form of entertainment.

13

Healthy Eating for Boys

Growing up involves eating the right foods. Some young people eat too little food, while others eat junk foods that do not nourish them. All these hurt your body.

Young boys, who indulge in unhealthy eating patterns often fall sick, become overweight or underweight.

Eating frequently is important. Try eating three or more meals a day, with one or two snacks in between.

Healthy eating helps your muscles to grow and develop.

It might be hard to focus in class when you skip breakfast. Taking breakfast boosts your brain's activities.

Your body is getting ready to go through a growth spurt, and it needs more food than usual to fuel that growth spurt.

Balanced diet contains all the six classes of food taken in the right proportion. A balanced diet is needed in this stage of your life. Remember, your body is making use of the resources it can get very fast to make you grow and mature into a full adult.

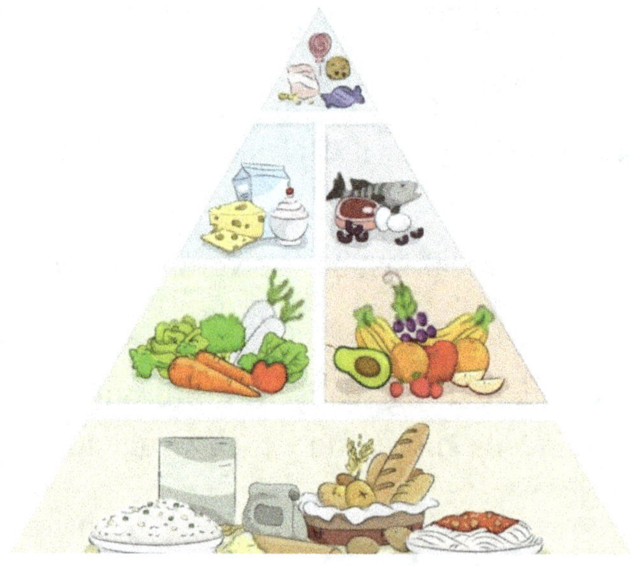

Your daily meals should contain the following:

1. Grains

Eating whole grains such as cereals and pasta. They give the energy needed by the body cells to do their work, and they are also good sources of fibres that aid in the digestion of food. Whole-grain foods are much better than non-whole-grain foods.   Eat about 6 ounces of grains per day. This is equivalent to 1 slice of bread, 1 cup of cereal, or a half-cup of pasta.

Vegetables are good sources of vitamins. They help you grow properly. Choose a wide variety of vegetables to ensure that you are getting a broad range of vitamins.

also, eat about two and a half cups of vegetables per day.

Fruits.

Fruits contain various vitamins that your body's cells, tissues, and organs require to produce the essential materials needed for your proper growth. Citrus for instance contains vitamin C. Grab a piece of fruit when you want a sweet snack- it has lots more nutrition than synthesized juice. Also, take about one and a half cups of fruits a day of fruits.

Milk.

Milk is high in proteins which build the body and Calcium which helps to build and maintain strong, healthy bones. take about 3 cups of milk a day.

Note:

that some people are lactose intolerant. This means that their genetic makeup does not enable them to break down lactose, a sugar present in milk. This causes constipation.

In addition, there are non-diary alternatives to milk where you can get proteins. This includes soymilk, among other things.

Meats and Beans.

Beans and meat are proteins. Proteins help to build the body and repair worn-out tissues. While beans are plant proteins because they are obtained from plants, meats are referred to as animal proteins because they are obtained from animals. Eat about 5 ounces of meat and beans a day. Three ounces of meat is the size of a deck of cards.

Oils.

Oils from fish, nuts and liquid oils (like palm oil and groundnut oil) are also good sources of minerals and energy. They should, however, be taken in moderation.

You are Awesome

Every day write something you appreciate about yourself on a piece of paper.

Then place it in a jar. You can decorate this jar however you want to make it fun and unique for them to have. You can open the jar at the end of each week or every two weeks (you choose) and read all of the nice things your kids wrote about themselves.

What an Amazing Journey

The end